This log book belongs to:

_____

Visit us at:
www.caregivinggracefully.com

EMERGENCY CONTACT LIST

Name:
_____ _____

Address:
_____ _____

Contact Number/s: Email:
_____ _____

Fax Number:
_____ _____

Name:
_____ _____

Address:
_____ _____

Contact Number/s: Email:
_____ _____

Fax Number
_____ _____

Name:
_____ _____

Address:
_____ _____

Contact Number/s: Email:
_____ _____

Fax Number
_____ _____

Name:
_____ _____

Address:
_____ _____

Contact Number/s: Email:
_____ _____

Fax Number:
_____ _____

EMERGENCY CONTACT LIST

Name:

Address:

Contact Number/s:

Email:

Fax Number:

Name:

Address:

Contact Number/s:

Email:

Fax Number

Name:

Address:

Contact Number/s:

Email:

Fax Number

Name:

Address:

Contact Number/s:

Email:

Fax Number:

DAILY LOG

Date: _____

SUPPLIES NEEDED

NOTES
_____
_____
_____
_____
_____

WATER/FLUIDS
○ ○ ○ ○
○ ○ ○ ○

APPOINTMENTS

BEHAVIORS/MOOD/SLEEP
_____
_____
_____
_____

MEALS:
BREAKFAST

LUNCH

VITAL SIGNS
BP

HR

Temp

Resp

O2

MEDICATIONS
_____
_____
_____
_____
_____
_____
_____
_____
_____
_____
_____
_____
_____

DINNER

TOILETING
Urine

BM

BLOOD SUGARS
AM

NOON

PM

BEDTIME

DAILY LOG

Date: _____

SUPPLIES NEEDED

APPOINTMENTS

VITAL SIGNS

BP

HR

Temp

Resp

O2

BLOOD SUGARS

AM

NOON

PM

BEDTIME

NOTES

_____
_____
_____
_____
_____

BEHAVIORS/MOOD/SLEEP

_____
_____
_____
_____

MEDICATIONS

_____
_____
_____
_____
_____
_____
_____
_____
_____
_____
_____
_____

WATER/FLUIDS

◯ ◯ ◯ ◯
◯ ◯ ◯ ◯

MEALS:

BREAKFAST

LUNCH

DINNER

TOILETING

Urine

BM

DAILY LOG

Date: _____

SUPPLIES NEEDED

APPOINTMENTS

VITAL SIGNS

BP

HR

Temp

Resp

O2

BLOOD SUGARS

AM

NOON

PM

BEDTIME

NOTES

_____
_____
_____
_____
_____

BEHAVIORS/MOOD/SLEEP

_____
_____
_____

MEDICATIONS

_____
_____
_____
_____
_____
_____
_____
_____
_____
_____
_____
_____
_____

WATER/FLUIDS

◯ ◯ ◯ ◯
◯ ◯ ◯ ◯

MEALS:

BREAKFAST

LUNCH

DINNER

TOILETING

Urine

BM

DAILY LOG

Date: _____

SUPPLIES NEEDED

APPOINTMENTS

VITAL SIGNS
BP

HR

Temp

Resp

O2

BLOOD SUGARS
AM

NOON

PM

BEDTIME

NOTES
_____
_____
_____
_____
_____

BEHAVIORS/MOOD/SLEEP
_____
_____
_____
_____

MEDICATIONS
_____
_____
_____
_____
_____
_____
_____
_____
_____
_____
_____

WATER/FLUIDS
○ ○ ○ ○
○ ○ ○ ○

MEALS:
BREAKFAST

LUNCH

DINNER

TOILETING
Urine

BM

DAILY LOG

Date: _____

SUPPLIES NEEDED

APPOINTMENTS

VITAL SIGNS
BP

HR

Temp

Resp

O2

BLOOD SUGARS
AM

NOON

PM

BEDTIME

NOTES
_____
_____
_____
_____
_____

BEHAVIORS/MOOD/SLEEP
_____
_____
_____
_____

MEDICATIONS
_____
_____
_____
_____
_____
_____
_____
_____
_____
_____
_____

WATER/FLUIDS
◯ ◯ ◯ ◯
◯ ◯ ◯ ◯

MEALS:
BREAKFAST

LUNCH

DINNER

TOILETING
Urine

BM

DAILY LOG

Date: _____

SUPPLIES NEEDED

APPOINTMENTS

VITAL SIGNS
BP

HR

Temp

Resp

O2

BLOOD SUGARS
AM

NOON

PM

BEDTIME

NOTES
_____
_____
_____
_____
_____

BEHAVIORS/MOOD/SLEEP
_____
_____
_____
_____

MEDICATIONS
_____
_____
_____
_____
_____
_____
_____
_____
_____
_____
_____
_____

WATER/FLUIDS
◯ ◯ ◯ ◯
◯ ◯ ◯ ◯

MEALS:
BREAKFAST

LUNCH

DINNER

TOILETING
Urine

BM

DAILY LOG

Date: _____

SUPPLIES NEEDED

NOTES
_____
_____
_____
_____
_____

WATER/FLUIDS
◯ ◯ ◯ ◯
◯ ◯ ◯ ◯

APPOINTMENTS

BEHAVIORS/MOOD/SLEEP
_____
_____
_____
_____

MEALS:

BREAKFAST

VITAL SIGNS

BP

HR

Temp

Resp

O2

MEDICATIONS
_____
_____
_____
_____
_____
_____
_____
_____
_____
_____
_____
_____
_____

LUNCH

DINNER

TOILETING

Urine

BLOOD SUGARS

AM

NOON

PM

BEDTIME

BM

DAILY LOG

Date: _____

SUPPLIES NEEDED

APPOINTMENTS

VITAL SIGNS
BP

HR

Temp

Resp

O2

BLOOD SUGARS
AM

NOON

PM

BEDTIME

NOTES
_____
_____
_____
_____
_____

BEHAVIORS/MOOD/SLEEP
_____
_____
_____
_____

MEDICATIONS
_____
_____
_____
_____
_____
_____
_____
_____
_____
_____
_____
_____

WATER/FLUIDS
◯ ◯ ◯ ◯
◯ ◯ ◯ ◯

MEALS:

BREAKFAST

LUNCH

DINNER

TOILETING
Urine

BM

DAILY LOG

Date: _____

SUPPLIES NEEDED

APPOINTMENTS

VITAL SIGNS
BP

HR

Temp

Resp

O2

BLOOD SUGARS
AM

NOON

PM

BEDTIME

NOTES
_____
_____
_____
_____
_____

BEHAVIORS/MOOD/SLEEP
_____
_____
_____
_____

MEDICATIONS
_____
_____
_____
_____
_____
_____
_____
_____
_____
_____
_____
_____
_____

WATER/FLUIDS
○ ○ ○ ○
○ ○ ○ ○

MEALS:
BREAKFAST

LUNCH

DINNER

TOILETING
Urine

BM

DAILY LOG

Date: _____

SUPPLIES NEEDED

APPOINTMENTS

VITAL SIGNS
BP

HR

Temp

Resp

O2

BLOOD SUGARS
AM

NOON

PM

BEDTIME

NOTES
_____
_____
_____
_____
_____

BEHAVIORS/MOOD/SLEEP
_____
_____
_____
_____

MEDICATIONS
_____
_____
_____
_____
_____
_____
_____
_____
_____
_____
_____
_____
_____
_____

WATER/FLUIDS
○ ○ ○ ○
○ ○ ○ ○

MEALS:
BREAKFAST

LUNCH

DINNER

TOILETING
Urine

BM

DAILY LOG

Date: _____

SUPPLIES NEEDED

APPOINTMENTS

VITAL SIGNS

BP

HR

Temp

Resp

O2

BLOOD SUGARS

AM

NOON

PM

BEDTIME

NOTES

_____
_____
_____
_____
_____

BEHAVIORS/MOOD/SLEEP

_____
_____
_____
_____

MEDICATIONS

_____
_____
_____
_____
_____
_____
_____
_____
_____
_____
_____
_____
_____

WATER/FLUIDS

○ ○ ○ ○
○ ○ ○ ○

MEALS:

BREAKFAST

LUNCH

DINNER

TOILETING

Urine

BM

DAILY LOG

Date: _____

SUPPLIES NEEDED

APPOINTMENTS

VITAL SIGNS
BP

HR

Temp

Resp

O2

BLOOD SUGARS
AM

NOON

PM

BEDTIME

NOTES
_____
_____
_____
_____
_____

BEHAVIORS/MOOD/SLEEP
_____
_____
_____
_____

MEDICATIONS
_____
_____
_____
_____
_____
_____
_____
_____
_____
_____
_____

WATER/FLUIDS
○ ○ ○ ○
○ ○ ○ ○

MEALS:
BREAKFAST

LUNCH

DINNER

TOILETING
Urine

BM

DAILY LOG

Date: _____

SUPPLIES NEEDED

APPOINTMENTS

VITAL SIGNS

BP

HR

Temp

Resp

O2

BLOOD SUGARS

AM

NOON

PM

BEDTIME

NOTES

_____
_____
_____
_____
_____

BEHAVIORS/MOOD/SLEEP

_____
_____
_____
_____

MEDICATIONS

_____
_____
_____
_____
_____
_____
_____
_____
_____
_____
_____
_____

WATER/FLUIDS

◯ ◯ ◯ ◯
◯ ◯ ◯ ◯

MEALS:

BREAKFAST

LUNCH

DINNER

TOILETING

Urine

BM

DAILY LOG

Date: _____

SUPPLIES NEEDED

APPOINTMENTS

VITAL SIGNS

BP

HR

Temp

Resp

O2

BLOOD SUGARS

AM

NOON

PM

BEDTIME

NOTES

_____
_____
_____
_____
_____

BEHAVIORS/MOOD/SLEEP

_____
_____
_____
_____

MEDICATIONS

_____
_____
_____
_____
_____
_____
_____
_____
_____
_____

WATER/FLUIDS

○ ○ ○ ○
○ ○ ○ ○

MEALS:

BREAKFAST

LUNCH

DINNER

TOILETING

Urine

BM

DAILY LOG

Date: _____

SUPPLIES NEEDED

APPOINTMENTS

VITAL SIGNS

BP

HR

Temp

Resp

O2

BLOOD SUGARS

AM

NOON

PM

BEDTIME

NOTES

_____
_____
_____
_____
_____

BEHAVIORS/MOOD/SLEEP

_____
_____
_____
_____

MEDICATIONS

_____
_____
_____
_____
_____
_____
_____
_____
_____
_____
_____
_____
_____

WATER/FLUIDS

◯ ◯ ◯ ◯
◯ ◯ ◯ ◯

MEALS:

BREAKFAST

LUNCH

DINNER

TOILETING

Urine

BM

DAILY LOG

Date: _____

SUPPLIES NEEDED

APPOINTMENTS

VITAL SIGNS
BP

HR

Temp

Resp

O2

BLOOD SUGARS
AM

NOON

PM

BEDTIME

NOTES
_____
_____
_____
_____
_____

BEHAVIORS/MOOD/SLEEP
_____
_____
_____
_____

MEDICATIONS
_____
_____
_____
_____
_____
_____
_____
_____
_____
_____
_____
_____
_____

WATER/FLUIDS
◯ ◯ ◯ ◯
◯ ◯ ◯ ◯

MEALS:

BREAKFAST

LUNCH

DINNER

TOILETING

Urine

BM

DAILY LOG

Date: _____

SUPPLIES NEEDED

APPOINTMENTS

VITAL SIGNS
BP

HR

Temp

Resp

O2

BLOOD SUGARS
AM

NOON

PM

BEDTIME

NOTES
_____
_____
_____
_____
_____

BEHAVIORS/MOOD/SLEEP
_____
_____
_____
_____

MEDICATIONS
_____
_____
_____
_____
_____
_____
_____
_____
_____
_____
_____

WATER/FLUIDS
○ ○ ○ ○
○ ○ ○ ○

MEALS:
BREAKFAST

LUNCH

DINNER

TOILETING
Urine

BM

DAILY LOG

Date: _____

SUPPLIES NEEDED

APPOINTMENTS

VITAL SIGNS
BP

HR

Temp

Resp

O2

BLOOD SUGARS
AM

NOON

PM

BEDTIME

NOTES
_____
_____
_____
_____
_____

BEHAVIORS/MOOD/SLEEP
_____
_____
_____
_____

MEDICATIONS
_____
_____
_____
_____
_____
_____
_____
_____
_____
_____
_____
_____

WATER/FLUIDS
◯ ◯ ◯ ◯
◯ ◯ ◯ ◯

MEALS:
BREAKFAST

LUNCH

DINNER

TOILETING
Urine

BM

DAILY LOG

Date: _____

SUPPLIES NEEDED

NOTES

_____
_____
_____
_____
_____
_____

WATER/FLUIDS

◯ ◯ ◯ ◯
◯ ◯ ◯ ◯

APPOINTMENTS

BEHAVIORS/MOOD/SLEEP

_____
_____
_____
_____

MEALS:

BREAKFAST

LUNCH

VITAL SIGNS

BP

HR

Temp

Resp

O2

MEDICATIONS

_____
_____
_____
_____
_____
_____
_____
_____
_____
_____
_____
_____
_____

DINNER

TOILETING

Urine

BLOOD SUGARS

AM

NOON

PM

BEDTIME

BM

DAILY LOG

Date: _____

SUPPLIES NEEDED

NOTES
_____
_____
_____
_____
_____

WATER/FLUIDS
◯ ◯ ◯ ◯
◯ ◯ ◯ ◯

APPOINTMENTS

BEHAVIORS/MOOD/SLEEP
_____
_____
_____
_____

MEALS:

BREAKFAST

LUNCH

DINNER

VITAL SIGNS

BP

HR

Temp

Resp

O2

MEDICATIONS
_____
_____
_____
_____
_____
_____
_____
_____
_____
_____
_____
_____

BLOOD SUGARS

AM

NOON

PM

BEDTIME

TOILETING

Urine

BM

DAILY LOG

Date: _____

SUPPLIES NEEDED

APPOINTMENTS

VITAL SIGNS

BP

HR

Temp

Resp

O2

BLOOD SUGARS

AM

NOON

PM

BEDTIME

NOTES

_____
_____
_____
_____
_____

BEHAVIORS/MOOD/SLEEP

_____
_____
_____
_____

MEDICATIONS

_____
_____
_____
_____
_____
_____
_____
_____
_____
_____
_____
_____

WATER/FLUIDS

◯ ◯ ◯ ◯
◯ ◯ ◯ ◯

MEALS:

BREAKFAST

LUNCH

DINNER

TOILETING

Urine

BM

DAILY LOG

Date: _____

SUPPLIES NEEDED

APPOINTMENTS

VITAL SIGNS
BP

HR

Temp

Resp

O2

BLOOD SUGARS
AM

NOON

PM

BEDTIME

NOTES
_____
_____
_____
_____
_____

BEHAVIORS/MOOD/SLEEP
_____
_____
_____
_____

MEDICATIONS
_____
_____
_____
_____
_____
_____
_____
_____
_____
_____
_____
_____

WATER/FLUIDS
○ ○ ○ ○
○ ○ ○ ○

MEALS:
BREAKFAST

LUNCH

DINNER

TOILETING
Urine

BM

DAILY LOG

Date: _____

SUPPLIES NEEDED

APPOINTMENTS

VITAL SIGNS
BP

HR

Temp

Resp

O2

BLOOD SUGARS
AM

NOON

PM

BEDTIME

NOTES
_____
_____
_____
_____
_____

BEHAVIORS/MOOD/SLEEP
_____
_____
_____
_____

MEDICATIONS
_____
_____
_____
_____
_____
_____
_____
_____
_____
_____
_____
_____

WATER/FLUIDS
◯ ◯ ◯ ◯
◯ ◯ ◯ ◯

MEALS:
BREAKFAST

LUNCH

DINNER

TOILETING
Urine

BM

DAILY LOG

Date: _____

SUPPLIES NEEDED

APPOINTMENTS

VITAL SIGNS
BP

HR

Temp

Resp

O2

BLOOD SUGARS
AM

NOON

PM

BEDTIME

NOTES
_____
_____
_____
_____
_____

BEHAVIORS/MOOD/SLEEP
_____
_____
_____
_____

MEDICATIONS
_____
_____
_____
_____
_____
_____
_____
_____
_____
_____
_____
_____

WATER/FLUIDS
○ ○ ○ ○
○ ○ ○ ○

MEALS:
BREAKFAST

LUNCH

DINNER

TOILETING
Urine

BM

DAILY LOG

Date: _____

SUPPLIES NEEDED

APPOINTMENTS

VITAL SIGNS
BP

HR

Temp

Resp

O2

BLOOD SUGARS
AM

NOON

PM

BEDTIME

NOTES
_____
_____
_____
_____
_____

BEHAVIORS/MOOD/SLEEP
_____
_____
_____
_____

MEDICATIONS
_____
_____
_____
_____
_____
_____
_____
_____
_____
_____
_____

WATER/FLUIDS
○ ○ ○ ○
○ ○ ○ ○

MEALS:
BREAKFAST

LUNCH

DINNER

TOILETING
Urine

BM

DAILY LOG

Date: _____

SUPPLIES NEEDED

APPOINTMENTS

VITAL SIGNS
BP

HR

Temp

Resp

O2

BLOOD SUGARS
AM

NOON

PM

BEDTIME

NOTES
_____
_____
_____
_____
_____

BEHAVIORS/MOOD/SLEEP
_____
_____
_____
_____

MEDICATIONS
_____
_____
_____
_____
_____
_____
_____
_____
_____
_____
_____
_____
_____
_____

WATER/FLUIDS
○ ○ ○ ○
○ ○ ○ ○

MEALS:
BREAKFAST

LUNCH

DINNER

TOILETING
Urine

BM

DAILY LOG

Date: _____

SUPPLIES NEEDED

NOTES
_____
_____
_____
_____
_____

WATER/FLUIDS
○ ○ ○ ○
○ ○ ○ ○

APPOINTMENTS

BEHAVIORS/MOOD/SLEEP
_____
_____
_____
_____

MEALS:

BREAKFAST

LUNCH

VITAL SIGNS

BP

HR

Temp

Resp

O2

MEDICATIONS
_____
_____
_____
_____
_____
_____
_____
_____
_____
_____
_____
_____

DINNER

TOILETING

Urine

BLOOD SUGARS

AM

NOON

PM

BEDTIME

BM

DAILY LOG

Date: _____

SUPPLIES NEEDED

NOTES
_____
_____
_____
_____
_____

WATER/FLUIDS
◯ ◯ ◯ ◯
◯ ◯ ◯ ◯

APPOINTMENTS

BEHAVIORS/MOOD/SLEEP
_____
_____
_____
_____

MEALS:

BREAKFAST

LUNCH

VITAL SIGNS

BP

HR

Temp

Resp

O2

MEDICATIONS
_____
_____
_____
_____
_____
_____
_____
_____
_____
_____
_____
_____

DINNER

TOILETING

Urine

BM

BLOOD SUGARS

AM

NOON

PM

BEDTIME

DAILY LOG

Date: _____

SUPPLIES NEEDED

APPOINTMENTS

VITAL SIGNS
BP

HR

Temp

Resp

O2

BLOOD SUGARS
AM

NOON

PM

BEDTIME

NOTES
_____
_____
_____
_____
_____

BEHAVIORS/MOOD/SLEEP
_____
_____
_____
_____

MEDICATIONS
_____
_____
_____
_____
_____
_____
_____
_____
_____
_____
_____
_____

WATER/FLUIDS
◯ ◯ ◯ ◯
◯ ◯ ◯ ◯

MEALS:
BREAKFAST

LUNCH

DINNER

TOILETING
Urine

BM

DAILY LOG

Date: _____

SUPPLIES NEEDED

APPOINTMENTS

VITAL SIGNS
BP

HR

Temp

Resp

O2

BLOOD SUGARS
AM

NOON

PM

BEDTIME

NOTES
_____
_____
_____
_____
_____

BEHAVIORS/MOOD/SLEEP
_____
_____
_____
_____

MEDICATIONS
_____
_____
_____
_____
_____
_____
_____
_____
_____
_____
_____
_____
_____

WATER/FLUIDS
○ ○ ○ ○
○ ○ ○ ○

MEALS:
BREAKFAST

LUNCH

DINNER

TOILETING
Urine

BM

DAILY LOG

Date: _____

SUPPLIES NEEDED

APPOINTMENTS

VITAL SIGNS

BP

HR

Temp

Resp

O2

BLOOD SUGARS

AM

NOON

PM

BEDTIME

NOTES

_____
_____
_____
_____
_____

BEHAVIORS/MOOD/SLEEP

_____
_____
_____
_____

MEDICATIONS

_____
_____
_____
_____
_____
_____
_____
_____
_____
_____
_____
_____
_____

WATER/FLUIDS

◯ ◯ ◯ ◯
◯ ◯ ◯ ◯

MEALS:

BREAKFAST

LUNCH

DINNER

TOILETING

Urine

BM

DAILY LOG

Date: _____

SUPPLIES NEEDED

APPOINTMENTS

VITAL SIGNS
BP

HR

Temp

Resp

O2

BLOOD SUGARS
AM

NOON

PM

BEDTIME

NOTES
_____
_____
_____
_____
_____

BEHAVIORS/MOOD/SLEEP
_____
_____
_____
_____

MEDICATIONS
_____
_____
_____
_____
_____
_____
_____
_____
_____
_____
_____
_____
_____
_____

WATER/FLUIDS
◯ ◯ ◯ ◯
◯ ◯ ◯ ◯

MEALS:
BREAKFAST

LUNCH

DINNER

TOILETING
Urine

BM

DAILY LOG

Date: _____

SUPPLIES NEEDED

APPOINTMENTS

VITAL SIGNS

BP

HR

Temp

Resp

O2

BLOOD SUGARS

AM

NOON

PM

BEDTIME

NOTES

_____
_____
_____
_____
_____

BEHAVIORS/MOOD/SLEEP

_____
_____
_____
_____

MEDICATIONS

_____
_____
_____
_____
_____
_____
_____
_____
_____
_____
_____

WATER/FLUIDS

◯ ◯ ◯ ◯
◯ ◯ ◯ ◯

MEALS:

BREAKFAST

LUNCH

DINNER

TOILETING

Urine

BM

DAILY LOG

Date: _____

SUPPLIES NEEDED

APPOINTMENTS

VITAL SIGNS

BP

HR

Temp

Resp

O2

BLOOD SUGARS

AM

NOON

PM

BEDTIME

NOTES

_____
_____
_____
_____
_____

BEHAVIORS/MOOD/SLEEP

_____
_____
_____
_____
_____

MEDICATIONS

_____
_____
_____
_____
_____
_____
_____
_____
_____
_____
_____
_____
_____

WATER/FLUIDS

○ ○ ○ ○
○ ○ ○ ○

MEALS:

BREAKFAST

LUNCH

DINNER

TOILETING

Urine

BM

DAILY LOG

Date: _____

SUPPLIES NEEDED

APPOINTMENTS

VITAL SIGNS

BP

HR

Temp

Resp

O2

BLOOD SUGARS

AM

NOON

PM

BEDTIME

NOTES

_____
_____
_____
_____
_____

BEHAVIORS/MOOD/SLEEP

_____
_____
_____
_____

MEDICATIONS

_____
_____
_____
_____
_____
_____
_____
_____
_____
_____
_____
_____

WATER/FLUIDS

◯ ◯ ◯ ◯
◯ ◯ ◯ ◯

MEALS:

BREAKFAST

LUNCH

DINNER

TOILETING

Urine

BM

DAILY LOG

Date: _____

SUPPLIES NEEDED

APPOINTMENTS

VITAL SIGNS
BP

HR

Temp

Resp

O2

BLOOD SUGARS
AM

NOON

PM

BEDTIME

NOTES
_____
_____
_____
_____
_____

BEHAVIORS/MOOD/SLEEP
_____
_____
_____
_____

MEDICATIONS
_____
_____
_____
_____
_____
_____
_____
_____
_____
_____
_____
_____

WATER/FLUIDS
◯ ◯ ◯ ◯
◯ ◯ ◯ ◯

MEALS:
BREAKFAST

LUNCH

DINNER

TOILETING
Urine

BM

DAILY LOG

Date: _____

SUPPLIES NEEDED

APPOINTMENTS

VITAL SIGNS
BP

HR

Temp

Resp

O2

BLOOD SUGARS
AM

NOON

PM

BEDTIME

NOTES
_____
_____
_____
_____
_____

BEHAVIORS/MOOD/SLEEP
_____
_____
_____
_____

MEDICATIONS
_____
_____
_____
_____
_____
_____
_____
_____
_____
_____
_____
_____

WATER/FLUIDS
◯ ◯ ◯ ◯
◯ ◯ ◯ ◯

MEALS:
BREAKFAST

LUNCH

DINNER

TOILETING
Urine

BM

DAILY LOG

Date: _____

SUPPLIES NEEDED

APPOINTMENTS

VITAL SIGNS

BP

HR

Temp

Resp

O2

BLOOD SUGARS

AM

NOON

PM

BEDTIME

NOTES

_____
_____
_____
_____
_____

BEHAVIORS/MOOD/SLEEP

_____
_____
_____
_____

MEDICATIONS

_____
_____
_____
_____
_____
_____
_____
_____
_____
_____
_____
_____

WATER/FLUIDS

◯ ◯ ◯ ◯
◯ ◯ ◯ ◯

MEALS:

BREAKFAST

LUNCH

DINNER

TOILETING

Urine

BM

DAILY LOG

Date: _____

SUPPLIES NEEDED

APPOINTMENTS

VITAL SIGNS
BP

HR

Temp

Resp

O2

BLOOD SUGARS
AM

NOON

PM

BEDTIME

NOTES
_____
_____
_____
_____
_____

BEHAVIORS/MOOD/SLEEP
_____
_____
_____
_____

MEDICATIONS
_____
_____
_____
_____
_____
_____
_____
_____
_____
_____
_____
_____
_____

WATER/FLUIDS
◯ ◯ ◯ ◯
◯ ◯ ◯ ◯

MEALS:
BREAKFAST

LUNCH

DINNER

TOILETING
Urine

BM

DAILY LOG

Date: _____

SUPPLIES NEEDED

APPOINTMENTS

VITAL SIGNS
BP

HR

Temp

Resp

O2

BLOOD SUGARS
AM

NOON

PM

BEDTIME

NOTES
_____
_____
_____
_____
_____

BEHAVIORS/MOOD/SLEEP
_____
_____
_____
_____

MEDICATIONS
_____
_____
_____
_____
_____
_____
_____
_____
_____
_____
_____
_____

WATER/FLUIDS
◯ ◯ ◯ ◯
◯ ◯ ◯ ◯

MEALS:

BREAKFAST

LUNCH

DINNER

TOILETING
Urine

BM

DAILY LOG

Date: _____

SUPPLIES NEEDED

APPOINTMENTS

VITAL SIGNS
BP

HR

Temp

Resp

O2

BLOOD SUGARS
AM

NOON

PM

BEDTIME

NOTES
_____
_____
_____
_____
_____
_____

BEHAVIORS/MOOD/SLEEP
_____
_____
_____
_____

MEDICATIONS
_____
_____
_____
_____
_____
_____
_____
_____
_____
_____
_____
_____

WATER/FLUIDS
○ ○ ○ ○
○ ○ ○ ○

MEALS:
BREAKFAST

LUNCH

DINNER

TOILETING
Urine

BM

DAILY LOG

Date: _____

SUPPLIES NEEDED

APPOINTMENTS

VITAL SIGNS

BP

HR

Temp

Resp

O2

BLOOD SUGARS

AM

NOON

PM

BEDTIME

NOTES

_____
_____
_____
_____
_____

BEHAVIORS/MOOD/SLEEP

_____
_____
_____
_____

MEDICATIONS

_____
_____
_____
_____
_____
_____
_____
_____
_____
_____
_____

WATER/FLUIDS

◯ ◯ ◯ ◯
◯ ◯ ◯ ◯

MEALS:

BREAKFAST

LUNCH

DINNER

TOILETING

Urine

BM

DAILY LOG

Date: _____

SUPPLIES NEEDED

APPOINTMENTS

VITAL SIGNS
BP

HR

Temp

Resp

O2

BLOOD SUGARS
AM

NOON

PM

BEDTIME

NOTES
_____
_____
_____
_____
_____
_____

BEHAVIORS/MOOD/SLEEP
_____
_____
_____
_____

MEDICATIONS
_____
_____
_____
_____
_____
_____
_____
_____
_____
_____
_____
_____

WATER/FLUIDS
◯ ◯ ◯ ◯
◯ ◯ ◯ ◯

MEALS:
BREAKFAST

LUNCH

DINNER

TOILETING
Urine

BM

DAILY LOG

Date: _____

SUPPLIES NEEDED

NOTES

_____
_____
_____
_____
_____

WATER/FLUIDS

◯ ◯ ◯ ◯
◯ ◯ ◯ ◯

APPOINTMENTS

BEHAVIORS/MOOD/SLEEP

_____
_____
_____
_____

MEALS:

BREAKFAST

LUNCH

VITAL SIGNS

BP

HR

Temp

Resp

O2

MEDICATIONS

_____
_____
_____
_____
_____
_____
_____
_____
_____
_____
_____
_____
_____
_____

DINNER

TOILETING

Urine

BLOOD SUGARS

AM

NOON

PM

BEDTIME

BM

DAILY LOG

Date: _____

SUPPLIES NEEDED

NOTES

_____
_____
_____
_____
_____

WATER/FLUIDS

○ ○ ○ ○
○ ○ ○ ○

APPOINTMENTS

BEHAVIORS/MOOD/SLEEP

_____
_____
_____
_____

MEALS:

BREAKFAST

LUNCH

DINNER

VITAL SIGNS

BP

HR

Temp

Resp

O2

MEDICATIONS

_____
_____
_____
_____
_____
_____
_____
_____
_____
_____
_____
_____

BLOOD SUGARS

AM

NOON

PM

BEDTIME

TOILETING

Urine

BM

DAILY LOG

Date: _____

SUPPLIES NEEDED

APPOINTMENTS

VITAL SIGNS
BP

HR

Temp

Resp

O2

BLOOD SUGARS
AM

NOON

PM

BEDTIME

NOTES
_____
_____
_____
_____
_____

BEHAVIORS/MOOD/SLEEP
_____
_____
_____
_____

MEDICATIONS
_____
_____
_____
_____
_____
_____
_____
_____
_____
_____
_____
_____
_____

WATER/FLUIDS
○ ○ ○ ○
○ ○ ○ ○

MEALS:
BREAKFAST

LUNCH

DINNER

TOILETING
Urine

BM

DAILY LOG

Date: _____

SUPPLIES NEEDED

APPOINTMENTS

VITAL SIGNS

BP

HR

Temp

Resp

O2

BLOOD SUGARS

AM

NOON

PM

BEDTIME

NOTES

_____
_____
_____
_____
_____

BEHAVIORS/MOOD/SLEEP

_____
_____
_____
_____

MEDICATIONS

_____
_____
_____
_____
_____
_____
_____
_____
_____
_____
_____
_____
_____

WATER/FLUIDS

◯ ◯ ◯ ◯
◯ ◯ ◯ ◯

MEALS:

BREAKFAST

LUNCH

DINNER

TOILETING

Urine

BM

DAILY LOG

Date: _____

SUPPLIES NEEDED

NOTES

_____
_____
_____
_____
_____

WATER/FLUIDS

◯ ◯ ◯ ◯
◯ ◯ ◯ ◯

APPOINTMENTS

BEHAVIORS/MOOD/SLEEP

_____
_____
_____
_____

MEALS:

BREAKFAST

LUNCH

VITAL SIGNS
BP

HR

Temp

Resp

O2

MEDICATIONS

_____
_____
_____
_____
_____
_____
_____
_____
_____
_____
_____
_____
_____

DINNER

TOILETING

Urine

BLOOD SUGARS
AM

NOON

PM

BEDTIME

BM

DAILY LOG

Date: _____

SUPPLIES NEEDED

APPOINTMENTS

VITAL SIGNS
BP

HR

Temp

Resp

O2

BLOOD SUGARS
AM

NOON

PM

BEDTIME

NOTES
_____
_____
_____
_____
_____
_____

BEHAVIORS/MOOD/SLEEP
_____
_____
_____
_____
_____

MEDICATIONS
_____
_____
_____
_____
_____
_____
_____
_____
_____
_____
_____
_____
_____

WATER/FLUIDS
○ ○ ○ ○
○ ○ ○ ○

MEALS:
BREAKFAST

LUNCH

DINNER

TOILETING
Urine

BM

DAILY LOG

Date: _____

SUPPLIES NEEDED

APPOINTMENTS

VITAL SIGNS

BP

HR

Temp

Resp

O2

BLOOD SUGARS

AM

NOON

PM

BEDTIME

NOTES

_____
_____
_____
_____
_____

BEHAVIORS/MOOD/SLEEP

_____
_____
_____
_____

MEDICATIONS

_____
_____
_____
_____
_____
_____
_____
_____
_____
_____
_____
_____

WATER/FLUIDS

◯ ◯ ◯ ◯
◯ ◯ ◯ ◯

MEALS:

BREAKFAST

LUNCH

DINNER

TOILETING

Urine

BM

DAILY LOG

Date: _____

SUPPLIES NEEDED

NOTES
_____
_____
_____
_____
_____

WATER/FLUIDS
○ ○ ○ ○
○ ○ ○ ○

APPOINTMENTS

BEHAVIORS/MOOD/SLEEP
_____
_____
_____
_____

MEALS:

BREAKFAST

VITAL SIGNS

BP

HR

Temp

Resp

O2

MEDICATIONS
_____
_____
_____
_____
_____
_____
_____
_____
_____
_____
_____
_____
_____

LUNCH

DINNER

TOILETING

Urine

BLOOD SUGARS

AM

NOON

PM

BEDTIME

BM

DAILY LOG

Date: _____

SUPPLIES NEEDED

APPOINTMENTS

VITAL SIGNS
BP

HR

Temp

Resp

O2

BLOOD SUGARS
AM

NOON

PM

BEDTIME

NOTES
_____
_____
_____
_____
_____

BEHAVIORS/MOOD/SLEEP
_____
_____
_____
_____

MEDICATIONS
_____
_____
_____
_____
_____
_____
_____
_____
_____
_____
_____
_____

WATER/FLUIDS
○ ○ ○ ○
○ ○ ○ ○

MEALS:
BREAKFAST

LUNCH

DINNER

TOILETING
Urine

BM

DAILY LOG

Date: _____

SUPPLIES NEEDED

APPOINTMENTS

VITAL SIGNS
BP

HR

Temp

Resp

O2

BLOOD SUGARS
AM

NOON

PM

BEDTIME

NOTES
_____
_____
_____
_____
_____

BEHAVIORS/MOOD/SLEEP
_____
_____
_____
_____

MEDICATIONS
_____
_____
_____
_____
_____
_____
_____
_____
_____
_____

WATER/FLUIDS
◯ ◯ ◯ ◯
◯ ◯ ◯ ◯

MEALS:
BREAKFAST

LUNCH

DINNER

TOILETING
Urine

BM

DAILY LOG

Date: _____

SUPPLIES NEEDED

APPOINTMENTS

VITAL SIGNS
BP

HR

Temp

Resp

O2

BLOOD SUGARS
AM

NOON

PM

BEDTIME

NOTES
_____
_____
_____
_____
_____

BEHAVIORS/MOOD/SLEEP
_____
_____
_____
_____

MEDICATIONS
_____
_____
_____
_____
_____
_____
_____
_____
_____
_____
_____
_____
_____

WATER/FLUIDS
◯ ◯ ◯ ◯
◯ ◯ ◯ ◯

MEALS:
BREAKFAST

LUNCH

DINNER

TOILETING
Urine

BM

DAILY LOG

Date: _____

SUPPLIES NEEDED

APPOINTMENTS

VITAL SIGNS
BP

HR

Temp

Resp

O2

BLOOD SUGARS
AM

NOON

PM

BEDTIME

NOTES
_____
_____
_____
_____
_____

BEHAVIORS/MOOD/SLEEP
_____
_____
_____

MEDICATIONS
_____
_____
_____
_____
_____
_____
_____
_____
_____
_____
_____

WATER/FLUIDS
◯ ◯ ◯ ◯
◯ ◯ ◯ ◯

MEALS:
BREAKFAST

LUNCH

DINNER

TOILETING
Urine

BM

DAILY LOG

Date: _____

SUPPLIES NEEDED

APPOINTMENTS

VITAL SIGNS
BP

HR

Temp

Resp

O2

BLOOD SUGARS
AM

NOON

PM

BEDTIME

NOTES
_____
_____
_____
_____
_____

BEHAVIORS/MOOD/SLEEP
_____
_____
_____
_____

MEDICATIONS
_____
_____
_____
_____
_____
_____
_____
_____
_____
_____
_____

WATER/FLUIDS
◯ ◯ ◯ ◯
◯ ◯ ◯ ◯

MEALS:
BREAKFAST

LUNCH

DINNER

TOILETING
Urine

BM

DAILY LOG

Date: _____

SUPPLIES NEEDED

APPOINTMENTS

VITAL SIGNS
BP

HR

Temp

Resp

O2

BLOOD SUGARS
AM

NOON

PM

BEDTIME

NOTES
_____
_____
_____
_____

BEHAVIORS/MOOD/SLEEP
_____
_____
_____
_____

MEDICATIONS
_____
_____
_____
_____
_____
_____
_____
_____
_____
_____
_____

WATER/FLUIDS
◯ ◯ ◯ ◯
◯ ◯ ◯ ◯

MEALS:
BREAKFAST

LUNCH

DINNER

TOILETING
Urine

BM

DAILY LOG

Date: _____

SUPPLIES NEEDED

APPOINTMENTS

VITAL SIGNS
BP

HR

Temp

Resp

O2

BLOOD SUGARS
AM

NOON

PM

BEDTIME

NOTES
_____
_____
_____
_____
_____

BEHAVIORS/MOOD/SLEEP
_____
_____
_____
_____

MEDICATIONS
_____
_____
_____
_____
_____
_____
_____
_____
_____
_____
_____
_____

WATER/FLUIDS
◯ ◯ ◯ ◯
◯ ◯ ◯ ◯

MEALS:
BREAKFAST

LUNCH

DINNER

TOILETING
Urine

BM

DAILY LOG

Date: _____

SUPPLIES NEEDED

APPOINTMENTS

VITAL SIGNS

BP

HR

Temp

Resp

O2

BLOOD SUGARS

AM

NOON

PM

BEDTIME

NOTES

_____
_____
_____
_____
_____

BEHAVIORS/MOOD/SLEEP

_____
_____
_____
_____

MEDICATIONS

_____
_____
_____
_____
_____
_____
_____
_____
_____
_____
_____
_____

WATER/FLUIDS

◯ ◯ ◯ ◯
◯ ◯ ◯ ◯

MEALS:

BREAKFAST

LUNCH

DINNER

TOILETING

Urine

BM

DAILY LOG

Date: _____

SUPPLIES NEEDED

APPOINTMENTS

VITAL SIGNS
BP

HR

Temp

Resp

O2

BLOOD SUGARS
AM

NOON

PM

BEDTIME

NOTES
_____
_____
_____
_____
_____
_____

BEHAVIORS/MOOD/SLEEP
_____
_____
_____
_____
_____

MEDICATIONS
_____
_____
_____
_____
_____
_____
_____
_____
_____
_____
_____
_____
_____
_____
_____

WATER/FLUIDS
○ ○ ○ ○
○ ○ ○ ○

MEALS:

BREAKFAST

LUNCH

DINNER

TOILETING
Urine

BM

DAILY LOG

Date: _____

SUPPLIES NEEDED

APPOINTMENTS

VITAL SIGNS
BP

HR

Temp

Resp

O2

BLOOD SUGARS
AM

NOON

PM

BEDTIME

NOTES
_____
_____
_____
_____
_____
_____

BEHAVIORS/MOOD/SLEEP
_____
_____
_____
_____
_____

MEDICATIONS
_____
_____
_____
_____
_____
_____
_____
_____
_____
_____
_____
_____
_____

WATER/FLUIDS
◯ ◯ ◯ ◯
◯ ◯ ◯ ◯

MEALS:
BREAKFAST

LUNCH

DINNER

TOILETING
Urine

BM

DAILY LOG

Date: _____

SUPPLIES NEEDED

APPOINTMENTS

VITAL SIGNS
BP

HR

Temp

Resp

O2

BLOOD SUGARS
AM

NOON

PM

BEDTIME

NOTES
_____
_____
_____
_____
_____

BEHAVIORS/MOOD/SLEEP
_____
_____
_____
_____

MEDICATIONS
_____
_____
_____
_____
_____
_____
_____
_____
_____
_____
_____
_____
_____

WATER/FLUIDS
○ ○ ○ ○
○ ○ ○ ○

MEALS:
BREAKFAST

LUNCH

DINNER

TOILETING
Urine

BM

DAILY LOG

Date: _____

SUPPLIES NEEDED

NOTES

_____
_____
_____
_____
_____

WATER/FLUIDS

◯ ◯ ◯ ◯
◯ ◯ ◯ ◯

APPOINTMENTS

BEHAVIORS/MOOD/SLEEP

_____
_____
_____
_____

MEALS:

BREAKFAST

LUNCH

VITAL SIGNS

BP

HR

Temp

Resp

O2

MEDICATIONS

_____
_____
_____
_____
_____
_____
_____
_____
_____
_____
_____
_____
_____
_____

DINNER

TOILETING

Urine

BLOOD SUGARS

AM

NOON

PM

BEDTIME

BM

DAILY LOG

Date: _____

SUPPLIES NEEDED

NOTES
_____
_____
_____
_____
_____

WATER/FLUIDS
○ ○ ○ ○
○ ○ ○ ○

APPOINTMENTS

BEHAVIORS/MOOD/SLEEP
_____
_____
_____
_____

MEALS:

BREAKFAST

LUNCH

VITAL SIGNS

BP

HR

Temp

Resp

O2

MEDICATIONS
_____
_____
_____
_____
_____
_____
_____
_____
_____
_____
_____
_____
_____
_____
_____

DINNER

TOILETING

Urine

BLOOD SUGARS

AM

NOON

PM

BEDTIME

BM

DAILY LOG

Date: _____

SUPPLIES NEEDED

APPOINTMENTS

VITAL SIGNS
BP

HR

Temp

Resp

O2

BLOOD SUGARS
AM

NOON

PM

BEDTIME

NOTES
_____
_____
_____
_____
_____

BEHAVIORS/MOOD/SLEEP
_____
_____
_____
_____

MEDICATIONS
_____
_____
_____
_____
_____
_____
_____
_____
_____
_____
_____

WATER/FLUIDS
◯ ◯ ◯ ◯
◯ ◯ ◯ ◯

MEALS:
BREAKFAST

LUNCH

DINNER

TOILETING
Urine

BM

DAILY LOG

Date: _____

SUPPLIES NEEDED

APPOINTMENTS

VITAL SIGNS

BP

HR

Temp

Resp

O2

BLOOD SUGARS

AM

NOON

PM

BEDTIME

NOTES

_____
_____
_____
_____
_____

BEHAVIORS/MOOD/SLEEP

_____
_____
_____
_____

MEDICATIONS

_____
_____
_____
_____
_____
_____
_____
_____
_____
_____
_____
_____

WATER/FLUIDS

◯ ◯ ◯ ◯
◯ ◯ ◯ ◯

MEALS:

BREAKFAST

LUNCH

DINNER

TOILETING

Urine

BM

DAILY LOG

Date: _____

SUPPLIES NEEDED

APPOINTMENTS

VITAL SIGNS
BP

HR

Temp

Resp

O2

BLOOD SUGARS
AM

NOON

PM

BEDTIME

NOTES
_____
_____
_____
_____
_____

BEHAVIORS/MOOD/SLEEP
_____
_____
_____
_____

MEDICATIONS
_____
_____
_____
_____
_____
_____
_____
_____
_____
_____
_____
_____

WATER/FLUIDS
◯ ◯ ◯ ◯
◯ ◯ ◯ ◯

MEALS:
BREAKFAST

LUNCH

DINNER

TOILETING
Urine

BM

DAILY LOG

Date: _____

SUPPLIES NEEDED

APPOINTMENTS

VITAL SIGNS
BP

HR

Temp

Resp

O2

BLOOD SUGARS
AM

NOON

PM

BEDTIME

NOTES
_____
_____
_____
_____
_____

BEHAVIORS/MOOD/SLEEP
_____
_____
_____
_____

MEDICATIONS
_____
_____
_____
_____
_____
_____
_____
_____
_____
_____
_____
_____

WATER/FLUIDS
◯ ◯ ◯ ◯
◯ ◯ ◯ ◯

MEALS:
BREAKFAST

LUNCH

DINNER

TOILETING
Urine

BM

DAILY LOG

Date: _____

SUPPLIES NEEDED

APPOINTMENTS

VITAL SIGNS

BP

HR

Temp

Resp

O2

BLOOD SUGARS

AM

NOON

PM

BEDTIME

NOTES

_____
_____
_____
_____
_____

BEHAVIORS/MOOD/SLEEP

_____
_____
_____
_____

MEDICATIONS

_____
_____
_____
_____
_____
_____
_____
_____
_____
_____
_____
_____

WATER/FLUIDS

◯ ◯ ◯ ◯
◯ ◯ ◯ ◯

MEALS:

BREAKFAST

LUNCH

DINNER

TOILETING

Urine

BM

DAILY LOG

Date: _____

SUPPLIES NEEDED

APPOINTMENTS

VITAL SIGNS
BP

HR

Temp

Resp

O2

BLOOD SUGARS
AM

NOON

PM

BEDTIME

NOTES
_____
_____
_____
_____
_____

BEHAVIORS/MOOD/SLEEP
_____
_____
_____
_____
_____

MEDICATIONS
_____
_____
_____
_____
_____
_____
_____
_____
_____
_____
_____
_____
_____
_____

WATER/FLUIDS
○ ○ ○ ○
○ ○ ○ ○

MEALS:

BREAKFAST

LUNCH

DINNER

TOILETING
Urine

BM

DAILY LOG

Date: _____

SUPPLIES NEEDED

APPOINTMENTS

VITAL SIGNS

BP

HR

Temp

Resp

O2

BLOOD SUGARS

AM

NOON

PM

BEDTIME

NOTES

_____
_____
_____
_____
_____

BEHAVIORS/MOOD/SLEEP

_____
_____
_____
_____

MEDICATIONS

_____
_____
_____
_____
_____
_____
_____
_____
_____
_____
_____
_____

WATER/FLUIDS

◯ ◯ ◯ ◯
◯ ◯ ◯ ◯

MEALS:

BREAKFAST

LUNCH

DINNER

TOILETING

Urine

BM

DAILY LOG

Date: _____

SUPPLIES NEEDED

APPOINTMENTS

VITAL SIGNS
BP

HR

Temp

Resp

O2

BLOOD SUGARS
AM

NOON

PM

BEDTIME

NOTES
_____
_____
_____
_____
_____

BEHAVIORS/MOOD/SLEEP
_____
_____
_____
_____
_____

MEDICATIONS
_____
_____
_____
_____
_____
_____
_____
_____
_____
_____
_____
_____
_____

WATER/FLUIDS
◯ ◯ ◯ ◯
◯ ◯ ◯ ◯

MEALS:
BREAKFAST

LUNCH

DINNER

TOILETING
Urine

BM

DAILY LOG

Date: _____

SUPPLIES NEEDED

NOTES
_____
_____
_____
_____
_____

WATER/FLUIDS
◯ ◯ ◯ ◯
◯ ◯ ◯ ◯

APPOINTMENTS

BEHAVIORS/MOOD/SLEEP
_____
_____
_____
_____

MEALS:

BREAKFAST

LUNCH

DINNER

VITAL SIGNS

BP

HR

Temp

Resp

O2

MEDICATIONS
_____
_____
_____
_____
_____
_____
_____
_____
_____
_____
_____
_____

BLOOD SUGARS

AM

NOON

PM

BEDTIME

TOILETING

Urine

BM

DAILY LOG

Date: _____

SUPPLIES NEEDED

APPOINTMENTS

VITAL SIGNS
BP

HR

Temp

Resp

O2

BLOOD SUGARS
AM

NOON

PM

BEDTIME

NOTES
_____
_____
_____
_____
_____

BEHAVIORS/MOOD/SLEEP
_____
_____
_____
_____

MEDICATIONS
_____
_____
_____
_____
_____
_____
_____
_____
_____
_____
_____
_____
_____
_____

WATER/FLUIDS
◯ ◯ ◯ ◯
◯ ◯ ◯ ◯

MEALS:
BREAKFAST

LUNCH

DINNER

TOILETING
Urine

BM

DAILY LOG

Date: _____

SUPPLIES NEEDED

APPOINTMENTS

VITAL SIGNS
BP

HR

Temp

Resp

O2

BLOOD SUGARS
AM

NOON

PM

BEDTIME

NOTES
_____
_____
_____
_____
_____

BEHAVIORS/MOOD/SLEEP
_____
_____
_____
_____

MEDICATIONS
_____
_____
_____
_____
_____
_____
_____
_____
_____
_____
_____
_____

WATER/FLUIDS
◯ ◯ ◯ ◯
◯ ◯ ◯ ◯

MEALS:
BREAKFAST

LUNCH

DINNER

TOILETING
Urine

BM

DAILY LOG

Date: _____

SUPPLIES NEEDED

APPOINTMENTS

VITAL SIGNS
BP

HR

Temp

Resp

O2

BLOOD SUGARS
AM

NOON

PM

BEDTIME

NOTES
_____
_____
_____
_____
_____

BEHAVIORS/MOOD/SLEEP
_____
_____
_____
_____

MEDICATIONS
_____
_____
_____
_____
_____
_____
_____
_____
_____
_____
_____
_____

WATER/FLUIDS
○ ○ ○ ○
○ ○ ○ ○

MEALS:

BREAKFAST

LUNCH

DINNER

TOILETING

Urine

BM

DAILY LOG

Date: _____

SUPPLIES NEEDED

APPOINTMENTS

VITAL SIGNS
BP

HR

Temp

Resp

O2

BLOOD SUGARS
AM

NOON

PM

BEDTIME

NOTES
_____
_____
_____
_____
_____

BEHAVIORS/MOOD/SLEEP
_____
_____
_____
_____

MEDICATIONS
_____
_____
_____
_____
_____
_____
_____
_____
_____
_____
_____
_____
_____
_____

WATER/FLUIDS
○ ○ ○ ○
○ ○ ○ ○

MEALS:
BREAKFAST

LUNCH

DINNER

TOILETING
Urine

BM

DAILY LOG

Date: _____

SUPPLIES NEEDED

APPOINTMENTS

VITAL SIGNS
BP

HR

Temp

Resp

O2

BLOOD SUGARS
AM

NOON

PM

BEDTIME

NOTES
_____
_____
_____
_____
_____

BEHAVIORS/MOOD/SLEEP
_____
_____
_____
_____

MEDICATIONS
_____
_____
_____
_____
_____
_____
_____
_____
_____
_____
_____
_____

WATER/FLUIDS
◯ ◯ ◯ ◯
◯ ◯ ◯ ◯

MEALS:
BREAKFAST

LUNCH

DINNER

TOILETING
Urine

BM

DAILY LOG

Date: _____

SUPPLIES NEEDED

APPOINTMENTS

VITAL SIGNS
BP

HR

Temp

Resp

O2

BLOOD SUGARS
AM

NOON

PM

BEDTIME

NOTES
_____
_____
_____
_____
_____

BEHAVIORS/MOOD/SLEEP
_____
_____
_____
_____

MEDICATIONS
_____
_____
_____
_____
_____
_____
_____
_____
_____
_____
_____
_____
_____

WATER/FLUIDS
◯ ◯ ◯ ◯
◯ ◯ ◯ ◯

MEALS:
BREAKFAST

LUNCH

DINNER

TOILETING
Urine

BM

DAILY LOG

Date: _____

SUPPLIES NEEDED

APPOINTMENTS

VITAL SIGNS
BP

HR

Temp

Resp

O2

BLOOD SUGARS
AM

NOON

PM

BEDTIME

NOTES
_____
_____
_____
_____
_____

BEHAVIORS/MOOD/SLEEP
_____
_____
_____
_____

MEDICATIONS
_____
_____
_____
_____
_____
_____
_____
_____
_____
_____
_____
_____

WATER/FLUIDS
○ ○ ○ ○
○ ○ ○ ○

MEALS:
BREAKFAST

LUNCH

DINNER

TOILETING
Urine

BM

DAILY LOG

Date: _____

SUPPLIES NEEDED

NOTES
_____
_____
_____
_____
_____

WATER/FLUIDS
◯ ◯ ◯ ◯
◯ ◯ ◯ ◯

APPOINTMENTS

BEHAVIORS/MOOD/SLEEP
_____
_____
_____
_____
_____

MEALS:

BREAKFAST

LUNCH

VITAL SIGNS
BP

HR

Temp

Resp

O2

MEDICATIONS
_____
_____
_____
_____
_____
_____
_____
_____
_____
_____
_____
_____
_____

DINNER

TOILETING
Urine

BM

BLOOD SUGARS
AM

NOON

PM

BEDTIME

DAILY LOG

Date: _____

SUPPLIES NEEDED

APPOINTMENTS

VITAL SIGNS
BP

HR

Temp

Resp

O2

BLOOD SUGARS
AM

NOON

PM

BEDTIME

NOTES
_____
_____
_____
_____
_____

BEHAVIORS/MOOD/SLEEP
_____
_____
_____
_____

MEDICATIONS
_____
_____
_____
_____
_____
_____
_____
_____
_____
_____
_____
_____
_____
_____

WATER/FLUIDS
◯ ◯ ◯ ◯
◯ ◯ ◯ ◯

MEALS:
BREAKFAST

LUNCH

DINNER

TOILETING
Urine

BM

DAILY LOG

Date: _____

SUPPLIES NEEDED

APPOINTMENTS

VITAL SIGNS
BP

HR

Temp

Resp

O2

BLOOD SUGARS
AM

NOON

PM

BEDTIME

NOTES
_____
_____
_____
_____
_____

BEHAVIORS/MOOD/SLEEP
_____
_____
_____
_____

MEDICATIONS
_____
_____
_____
_____
_____
_____
_____
_____
_____
_____

WATER/FLUIDS
◯ ◯ ◯ ◯
◯ ◯ ◯ ◯

MEALS:
BREAKFAST

LUNCH

DINNER

TOILETING
Urine

BM

DAILY LOG

Date: _____

SUPPLIES NEEDED

APPOINTMENTS

VITAL SIGNS
BP

HR

Temp

Resp

O2

BLOOD SUGARS
AM

NOON

PM

BEDTIME

NOTES
_____
_____
_____
_____
_____

BEHAVIORS/MOOD/SLEEP
_____
_____
_____
_____

MEDICATIONS
_____
_____
_____
_____
_____
_____
_____
_____
_____
_____
_____
_____

WATER/FLUIDS
○ ○ ○ ○
○ ○ ○ ○

MEALS:
BREAKFAST

LUNCH

DINNER

TOILETING
Urine

BM

DAILY LOG

Date: _____

SUPPLIES NEEDED

APPOINTMENTS

VITAL SIGNS
BP

HR

Temp

Resp

O2

BLOOD SUGARS
AM

NOON

PM

BEDTIME

NOTES
_____
_____
_____
_____
_____

BEHAVIORS/MOOD/SLEEP
_____
_____
_____
_____
_____

MEDICATIONS
_____
_____
_____
_____
_____
_____
_____
_____
_____
_____
_____
_____

WATER/FLUIDS
◯ ◯ ◯ ◯
◯ ◯ ◯ ◯

MEALS:

BREAKFAST

LUNCH

DINNER

TOILETING
Urine

BM

DAILY LOG

Date: _____

SUPPLIES NEEDED

APPOINTMENTS

VITAL SIGNS
BP

HR

Temp

Resp

O2

BLOOD SUGARS
AM

NOON

PM

BEDTIME

NOTES
_____
_____
_____
_____
_____

BEHAVIORS/MOOD/SLEEP
_____
_____
_____
_____

MEDICATIONS
_____
_____
_____
_____
_____
_____
_____
_____
_____
_____
_____
_____

WATER/FLUIDS
◯ ◯ ◯ ◯
◯ ◯ ◯ ◯

MEALS:
BREAKFAST

LUNCH

DINNER

TOILETING
Urine

BM

DAILY LOG

Date: _____

SUPPLIES NEEDED

APPOINTMENTS

VITAL SIGNS

BP

HR

Temp

Resp

O2

BLOOD SUGARS

AM

NOON

PM

BEDTIME

NOTES

_____
_____
_____
_____
_____

BEHAVIORS/MOOD/SLEEP

_____
_____
_____
_____

MEDICATIONS

_____
_____
_____
_____
_____
_____
_____
_____
_____
_____
_____
_____
_____

WATER/FLUIDS

○ ○ ○ ○
○ ○ ○ ○

MEALS:

BREAKFAST

LUNCH

DINNER

TOILETING

Urine

BM

DAILY LOG

Date: _____

SUPPLIES NEEDED

APPOINTMENTS

VITAL SIGNS
BP

HR

Temp

Resp

O2

BLOOD SUGARS
AM

NOON

PM

BEDTIME

NOTES
_____
_____
_____
_____

BEHAVIORS/MOOD/SLEEP
_____
_____
_____
_____

MEDICATIONS
_____
_____
_____
_____
_____
_____
_____
_____
_____
_____

WATER/FLUIDS
◯ ◯ ◯ ◯
◯ ◯ ◯ ◯

MEALS:
BREAKFAST

LUNCH

DINNER

TOILETING
Urine

BM

DAILY LOG

Date: _____

SUPPLIES NEEDED

APPOINTMENTS

VITAL SIGNS
BP

HR

Temp

Resp

O2

BLOOD SUGARS
AM

NOON

PM

BEDTIME

NOTES
_____
_____
_____
_____
_____

BEHAVIORS/MOOD/SLEEP
_____
_____
_____
_____

MEDICATIONS
_____
_____
_____
_____
_____
_____
_____
_____
_____
_____
_____
_____
_____

WATER/FLUIDS
○ ○ ○ ○
○ ○ ○ ○

MEALS:
BREAKFAST

LUNCH

DINNER

TOILETING
Urine

BM

DAILY LOG

Date: _____

SUPPLIES NEEDED

APPOINTMENTS

VITAL SIGNS
BP

HR

Temp

Resp

O2

BLOOD SUGARS
AM

NOON

PM

BEDTIME

NOTES
_____
_____
_____
_____
_____

BEHAVIORS/MOOD/SLEEP
_____
_____
_____
_____

MEDICATIONS
_____
_____
_____
_____
_____
_____
_____
_____
_____
_____
_____
_____

WATER/FLUIDS
◯ ◯ ◯ ◯
◯ ◯ ◯ ◯

MEALS:
BREAKFAST

LUNCH

DINNER

TOILETING
Urine

BM

DAILY LOG

Date: _____

SUPPLIES NEEDED

APPOINTMENTS

VITAL SIGNS

BP

HR

Temp

Resp

O2

BLOOD SUGARS

AM

NOON

PM

BEDTIME

NOTES

_____
_____
_____
_____
_____

BEHAVIORS/MOOD/SLEEP

_____
_____
_____
_____

MEDICATIONS

_____
_____
_____
_____
_____
_____
_____
_____
_____
_____
_____
_____

WATER/FLUIDS

◯ ◯ ◯ ◯
◯ ◯ ◯ ◯

MEALS:

BREAKFAST

LUNCH

DINNER

TOILETING

Urine

BM

DAILY LOG

Date: _____

SUPPLIES NEEDED

APPOINTMENTS

VITAL SIGNS
BP

HR

Temp

Resp

O2

BLOOD SUGARS
AM

NOON

PM

BEDTIME

NOTES
_____
_____
_____
_____
_____

BEHAVIORS/MOOD/SLEEP
_____
_____
_____
_____

MEDICATIONS
_____
_____
_____
_____
_____
_____
_____
_____
_____
_____
_____
_____

WATER/FLUIDS
◯ ◯ ◯ ◯
◯ ◯ ◯ ◯

MEALS:
BREAKFAST

LUNCH

DINNER

TOILETING
Urine

BM

DAILY LOG

Date: _____

SUPPLIES NEEDED

APPOINTMENTS

VITAL SIGNS
BP

HR

Temp

Resp

O2

BLOOD SUGARS
AM

NOON

PM

BEDTIME

NOTES
_____
_____
_____
_____
_____

BEHAVIORS/MOOD/SLEEP
_____
_____
_____
_____

MEDICATIONS
_____
_____
_____
_____
_____
_____
_____
_____
_____
_____
_____

WATER/FLUIDS
◯ ◯ ◯ ◯
◯ ◯ ◯ ◯

MEALS:

BREAKFAST

LUNCH

DINNER

TOILETING

Urine

BM

DAILY LOG

Date: _____

SUPPLIES NEEDED

APPOINTMENTS

VITAL SIGNS

BP

HR

Temp

Resp

O2

BLOOD SUGARS

AM

NOON

PM

BEDTIME

NOTES

_____
_____
_____
_____
_____

BEHAVIORS/MOOD/SLEEP

_____
_____
_____
_____
_____

MEDICATIONS

_____
_____
_____
_____
_____
_____
_____
_____
_____
_____
_____
_____
_____

WATER/FLUIDS

◯ ◯ ◯ ◯
◯ ◯ ◯ ◯

MEALS:

BREAKFAST

LUNCH

DINNER

TOILETING

Urine

BM

DAILY LOG

Date: _____

SUPPLIES NEEDED

APPOINTMENTS

VITAL SIGNS

BP

HR

Temp

Resp

O2

BLOOD SUGARS

AM

NOON

PM

BEDTIME

NOTES

_____
_____
_____
_____
_____

BEHAVIORS/MOOD/SLEEP

_____
_____
_____
_____

MEDICATIONS

_____
_____
_____
_____
_____
_____
_____
_____
_____
_____
_____
_____
_____

WATER/FLUIDS

◯ ◯ ◯ ◯
◯ ◯ ◯ ◯

MEALS:

BREAKFAST

LUNCH

DINNER

TOILETING

Urine

BM

DAILY LOG

Date: _____

SUPPLIES NEEDED

APPOINTMENTS

VITAL SIGNS
BP

HR

Temp

Resp

O2

BLOOD SUGARS
AM

NOON

PM

BEDTIME

NOTES
_____
_____
_____
_____

BEHAVIORS/MOOD/SLEEP
_____
_____
_____
_____

MEDICATIONS
_____
_____
_____
_____
_____
_____
_____
_____
_____
_____
_____

WATER/FLUIDS
○ ○ ○ ○
○ ○ ○ ○

MEALS:

BREAKFAST

LUNCH

DINNER

TOILETING
Urine

BM

DAILY LOG

Date: _____

SUPPLIES NEEDED

NOTES

_____
_____
_____
_____
_____

WATER/FLUIDS

◯ ◯ ◯ ◯
◯ ◯ ◯ ◯

APPOINTMENTS

BEHAVIORS/MOOD/SLEEP

_____
_____
_____
_____

MEALS:

BREAKFAST

LUNCH

VITAL SIGNS

BP

HR

Temp

Resp

O2

MEDICATIONS

_____
_____
_____
_____
_____
_____
_____
_____
_____
_____
_____
_____

DINNER

TOILETING

Urine

BLOOD SUGARS

AM

NOON

PM

BEDTIME

BM

DAILY LOG

Date: _____

SUPPLIES NEEDED

APPOINTMENTS

VITAL SIGNS
BP

HR

Temp

Resp

O2

BLOOD SUGARS
AM

NOON

PM

BEDTIME

NOTES
_____
_____
_____
_____
_____

BEHAVIORS/MOOD/SLEEP
_____
_____
_____
_____

MEDICATIONS
_____
_____
_____
_____
_____
_____
_____
_____
_____
_____
_____
_____
_____

WATER/FLUIDS
○ ○ ○ ○
○ ○ ○ ○

MEALS:

BREAKFAST

LUNCH

DINNER

TOILETING

Urine

BM

Made in the USA
Monee, IL
02 April 2022